The
Battle
of
Cowan's Ford

GENERAL DAVIDSON'S STAND ON THE CATAWBA RIVER,
AND ITS PLACE IN NORTH CAROLINA HISTORY

Ottis C. Stonestreet IV

Acknowledgments

I wish to thank several people for their support in this project. My father I would like to thank first for instilling a love of history in me at an early age. A special thanks to Terry and Mike "Mick" Shinn for their continued support through the entire project. And a special thank you to Albert Spurr.

Finally, a word of great appreciation goes to Jan Blodgett and Sharon Byrd, archivists at Davidson College Library; and Paul Johnson of the British Archive. Without the support of these fine people, this work would not have been possible. Thank you all!

Dedication

This book is dedicated to my grandmother Nellie R. Stonestreet. She was a true lady, patriot, and long-time member of the Daughters of the American Revolution.

Contents

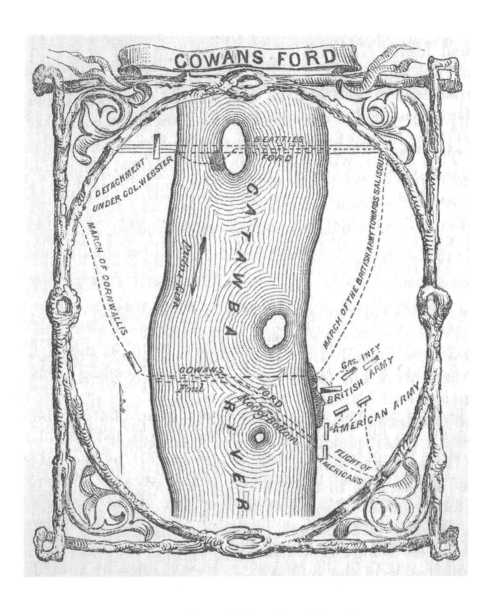

Courtesy of North Carolina Collection,
Wilson Special Collections Library, UNC-Chapel Hill

Introduction

The Battle of Cowan's Ford is but a footnote in the history of the American Revolutionary War in contrast to such famous battles as Concord, Bunker Hill or Yorktown. This is not surprising, because it is generally understood that for every major engagement in any conflict, many lesser-known "skirmishes" occurred. Some were never recorded and were lost to history once living memory faded. In truth, the Battle of Cowan's Ford is all but forgotten due to several reasons.[1]

First and foremost the fight was very short, less than an hour in length. The total number of combatants probably did not exceed more than several thousand. As a comparison from the American Civil War, the Battle of Gettysburg lasted three days and included some 160,000 participants.[2] Secondly, Cowan's Ford was a small engagement that happened between several larger and well-noted engagements. Lastly, due to influx of many people into the area in which the battle occurred, and thus the continued development over the last thirty years, local history is being erased as well as forgotten.

Even so, for a local historian the Battle of Cowan's Ford offers a chance to glimpse a skirmish set in the 18th Century. It is manageable as far as the numbers of participants, and the engagement site still remains. Most importantly, several primary accounts still exist that recorded the action on that dreary February morning of 1781. Yet, even these accounts differ on what actually occurred during the heat of battle. Few today, of the many thousands that currently reside along the banks of the Catawba River and its manmade Lake Norman, are aware that their picturesque community of rest and recreation was once the scene of desperate actions, heroics, and bloodshed over two centuries ago.

Setting the Stage: The Dawn of 1781

As the curtain fell on the year 1780, the world stage was being set for the war to enter its sixth agonizing year. A world stage indeed, for the American Revolutionary War was a conflict that now spanned much of the globe. The French, Spanish and Dutch Empires had become increasingly involved. Native American tribes as well could not sit idly by, and many had taken sides with either of the combatants, depending on the region. As one looks back across history from our current age, one can see that the revolutionary fires would continue to spread to another continent and burn after the flames of the American war continued to smolder in the autumn of 1781.

It is true that Britain faced the weight and might of a vengeful France as well as the ever tenacious "Rebels" in America. But to consider the war already won for the "American Cause" would be a great mistake. The battles of 1780 were brawls. Like two heavy weight boxers, both sides were staggering but "unwilling to throw in the towel." The British may have lost a major engagement at King's Mountain in October of 1780, but their earlier victories at Charleston and Camden ensured that they still maintained a strong grasp on South Carolina. The British still possessed a truly professional army, an empire with many resources, and a massive fleet to keep their forces well supplied. Lord Charles Cornwallis, the British commander, seemed to have a stronger determination for victory even in precarious circumstances. Flashes of "Napoleonic" ingenuity and zeal could be seen in Cornwallis. Most importantly, the American forces were still fleeing in the face of the British advance. Even with the stunning Patriot victory at Cowpens, the British doggedly pursued Morgan's forces. One or two more decisive victories in the American South for the British could change the entire course of the war yet again.

On December 2, 1780 Nathaniel Greene officially took command of the Southern theatre of operations from General Horatio Gates. Gates has, over time, taken somewhat of a historical pummeling for the performance of the forces under his command at Camden, South Carolina.[3] This should be considered a bit harsh, given that much of the Patriot forces located in the South were untried militia units.

As one will see, militia units react to military situations differently than regular forces; the responses of these militia units may have surprising results. Cowan's Ford is a prime example of the uncertainty of militia troops while facing a seasoned opponent. It was, indeed, a seasoned and motivated opponent that now moved ever towards the Catawba River at the end of January, 1781.

Cornwallis Cometh

The Battle of Cowan's Ford is a perfect case-study in what military historians call a "rearguard action." Essentially, this is when a smaller force is protecting the rear of a larger force which is in an orderly retreat or "tactical withdrawal." This defensive maneuver has but one objective, to "buy time." Unfortunately, many such rearguard actions in history have certain negative connotations. Names like Thermopylae, the Alamo, and Stalingrad come to mind when one thinks of the "few" holding back a large horde of their opponents.

General Daniel Morgan, that colorful old veteran and architect of the recent victory at Cowpens, was withdrawing his small force north in hopes of combining with other Patriot forces and finding fresh recruits in upper North Carolina. The trouble lay in the fact that Lord Cornwallis and several thousand professional British and German troops were moving as fast as possible to catch Morgan, and quite possibly apprehend the newly appointed commander of the American Army of the South, General Nathaniel Greene. In an act of determination to achieve this goal, Cornwallis had most of his baggage train burned, saving only the absolute necessities for a forced march. This was to lighten the load and thus hasten his pursuit of the Patriot forces only a few days ahead of him.[4] Cornwallis' famed "Race to the Dan River" thus starts in earnest.

As noted in the British Orderly Book, Lord Cornwallis knew the act of burning most of his supplies would cause great consternation among his officers and other ranks, but like any good commander, he also realized sacrifices in war must be made to achieve strategic goals: "Lord Cornwallis has so Often experience'd the Zeal & good Will of the Troops that he has not the Smallest doubt that the Offrs. & Soldiers will most Cheerfully Submit to the Ill Conveniences Which must Naturally attend a War so remote from Water carriage & the Magazines of the Army."[5]

While Lord Cornwallis broke camp at Ramsour's Mill on January 28th, General Greene had bolted over a hundred miles with a small escort to reach Beattie's Ford on January 31st.[6] At Beattie's, Greene met with General Morgan, Colonel William Washington, and the local militia leader Brigadier-General William Lee Davidson. To this day no one knows what exactly was said, for the men retired away from camp and sat on several fallen logs to discuss the strategic situation. Ironically, at that same moment a British reconnaissance force arrived on the opposite side of the river in plain sight of the conferring officers.[7] What can be ascertained from this conference is that while most of the Patriot forces headed for Salisbury, General Davidson and some eight hundred local militia were to make a stand on the Catawba. The delaying of Cornwallis's advance would greatly aid the withdrawal of the Southern Army, thus a classic "rearguard action."

The problem facing General Davidson was two-fold: First, where and when would his Lordship attempt a crossing? Second, how best to disperse his meager force for maximum effect against the British when they launch their attack? Davidson approached this tactical problem very methodically.

The British could choose from four possible fords across the Catawba: Toole's, Beattie's, Tuckasegee, and Cowan's. Due to recent heavy rains and the natural rise in the river during the early part of the year the Catawba was swollen, and the current was fast. Lord Cornwallis would probably have wanted to use Beattie's Ford as that it was reportedly the best ford on the river. However, his Lordship declined this crossing for two sensible reasons. First, Beattie's was a well-known public ford, and it would naturally be guarded. Second, the depth of the water and current, due to the recent weather, would most certainly damage his remaining wagons carrying salt and a heavy load of flour captured at Ramsour's Mills.[8] Naturally, he would have to seek a less-used yet very passable ford elsewhere. Cowan's was sensible as it was actually two fords in one, a general horse fording area and a wagon ford which lay a short distance (around one quarter-mile) down river.

As Davidson had seen British reconnaissance firsthand, he correctly estimated that Cornwallis would attempt a crossing within the next 48 hours. Leaving no ford unchecked, he decided to cover all of the fords relatively equally, and thus divided his force as such: two hundred men at Tuckasegee, seventy men at Toole's, two hundred-fifty at Beattie's, and two hundred-fifty at Cowan's Ford. To add to British difficulties, trees were felled as obstacles at both Tuckasegee and Toole's Ford.[9]

It is at this point that General Davidson took a tactical gamble that would affect all that followed. He reasoned that the British would not attempt the crossing at the rockier and deeper wagon ford at Cowan's, though it was a straighter path across the raging and swollen Catawba River. With the recent rains and the current, crossing at the wagon ford would be slow progress at best. Davidson thus concluded that Cornwallis would try the safest and quickest way possible to bring all his forces across the horse ford.

Having thought the matter through, Davidson left only a small picket of twenty-five men on the bank of the wagon ford exit under the command of a young relative Lieutenant Thomas Davidson.[10] General Davidson then established a main camp with the rest of his troops, some two hundred men of the Mecklenburg Militia under the command of Colonel William Polk, on a steep hill generally overlooking the horse ford exit.[11] Another small detachment of fifty local men acting as a cavalry contingent were to ride along the river's edge in the evening, for Morgan had warned Davidson that the enemy might try to send a detachment of cavalry over at night in order to cause trouble in the rear areas in anticipation of an early morning crossing.

From a layman's perspective, given the situation so far, it appears that General Davidson had positioned himself rather well. But upon closer study, one realizes that Davidson made several questionable decisions. First, with two hundred- fifty men, one could ask why did he not divide his force in half, having already committed a good number of his troops at Cowan's Ford? With the added help of the fast-moving Catawba and over a hundred guns brought to bear on any one crossing point, the British would be slowed enough so that the other half of Davidson's force could arrive in good order from either the horse or wagon exits. Major William Graham noted in his assessment of the battle that, " It would also seem that if the approach of the enemy could have been discerned in time to have place the militia at the wagon ford, they would have been seriously crippled if not defeated...."[12]

Interestingly enough, the archive at Davidson College has copies of General Davidson's personal letters. These letters were from Davidson's wallet which was taken from his body by the British following the engagement. The original contents of the wallet now reside in the British Archive and are still technically considered "trophies of war." In several of the letters, manpower and militia support were discussed in correspondences between Davidson and Generals Greene and Sumner just several weeks prior to the battle.[13]

While studying the letters, one quickly realizes that the lines of communication were actually quite good for the time due to the high quality of intelligence that is noted and the frequency of correspondences. Good evidence indicates that Davidson, like General Washington, had a strong network of spies. One scrap of paper has a very precise listing of troop numbers, specific regiments, and types of troops that were with Cornwallis as he approached Cowan's.[14]

One of the letters to General Greene dated January 16th, 1781 further discusses Lord Cornwallis' progress from Smith's Ford on the Broad River northward towards the Catawba, and Davidson's concerns over militia support, commenting that: " – Should Lord Cornwallis receive no reinforcements Gen. Morgan & Militia to be raised may render him very uneasy- I understand that a lot of Farmers from Hillsborough district is near at hand with about 200 Militia- should be glad to know if he is to join me." He then states, " I beg leave to suggest to you that it may be proper to send the guard in Training at Salisbury further to the North as they are consuming the resources of this country which are already far exhausted..."[15]

One can see that Davidson is already concerned about local support as Lord Cornwallis approached. Many of the men at Davidson's disposal on the Catawba were there because he had promised them three months militia service for six weeks active duty.[16] The question then is why would he want to have the questionable support of a few hundred local ill-trained farmers when he could have several hundred fairly well-trained militia from Salisbury within a few days? Furthermore, added numbers would allow a better dispersal of troops to all of the possible crossings that Cornwallis might take. Davidson suggested that there was a serious strain on resources, yet given the circumstances and the imminent British threat, would not any force (Hillsborough Militia or Salisbury Guards) be welcomed by the local populace; even with further strains on supplies?

One darker concern for the Patriots, though it is not voiced in any of the correspondence, was the existence of loyalist support in the region. In one of General Greene's communications to Lt. Colonel Hugins, Greene is definitely concerned about the apparent apathy that seemed pervasive at the time, "Davidson informs {me} he has called again and again for the people to turn out and defend their country. The inattention to his call and the backwardness among the people is unaccountable." [17] Many today forget that the British factored loyalist support (whether active or passive) as a positive point for waging a campaign in the American South.[18] As will be seen, a loyalist or "Tory" will play a part in the coming battle.

An interesting strategic point of note prior to the battle is Davidson's selected location for his main camp. It is estimated to have been between one-half to three-quarters of a mile away from either wagon or horse ford, thus placing his camp somewhat between the two.[19] One must remember that it was cool, lightly raining at times, and densely wooded. Even had General Davidson been correct and the British taken the horse ford, how well could his green militia perform having to load their weapons, run through the damp-dark morning, and then take unseen firing positions in time from some half-mile away? It is still not clear why he chose this location as his main camp. However, noting the possibility of drawing in an enemy cavalry screen during a night raid, it may have been perceived as a wise move at the time to have his camp located further from the river bank.

Naturally, it is easy to throw analytical stones two centuries in the future with the hindsight of history to help a person's aim. John Shy noted in his work, *A People Numerous & Armed,* that many of us may be overly critical in analyzing military leaders of the past: "We may hold high military commanders to an unrealistic, Napoleonic standard; when they fail to meet the standard, we may judge them too quickly as incompetents."[20] Shy may be right, however. General Davidson's actions at this critical point will still be debated by "armchair generals" for many years to come.

As it turns out a Davidson was the hero of the Battle of Cowan's Ford, but it was Lt. Thomas Davidson who showed some of the greatest leadership prior to the fight.[21] Lt. Davidson had his picket of twenty-five men choose their firing positions, and even ran readiness drills before night fell on January 31st, 1781. His men felt confident for the coming fight. Robert Henry, a local school boy of sixteen, remembered it as such: "I went to mine [firing position] and was well pleased with it-for in shooting, if I would miss my first aim, my lead would range along the British army obliquely and still do damage...."[22]

Lt. Davidson's men camped within a few yards of their positions with musket in hand to be ready for the coming action.

Unfortunately that night, whoever was selected to be on watch failed in his duty. At around one in the morning on February 1st, 1781, Lord

Cornwallis assembled his men and moved towards Cowan's Ford, led by a local Tory guide. The British lead elements were half-way across the river before anyone was aware of it. Militiaman Joel Jetton was awakened by the sounds of horses struggling in the current; he ran to the river's edge and kicked the sleeping sentry into the frigid water as he shouted, "The British! The British!" A shot alarmed the rest of the sleeping picketed men who were soon at their selected firing positions.[23]

Unknown to the men at Cowan's, much of the British artillery had moved to Beattie's Ford to fire several diversionary volleys. Cornwallis' force did have two-three pound cannons which could have been employed against the picket; and was actually seen by the Patriots prior to their crossing. Fortunately for the Patriots, all was going against Cornwallis at this point. One cannon overturned in marshy terrain, and the other was lost on the march due to breaks in the columns.[24] Cornwallis realized, even after seeing a sizable picket, that he must cross for fear that the rain, which was now beginning to become heavy, would certainly increase the river's flow and hinder a crossing later in the day.

The British were struggling against the river, and as the lead elements crossed the half-way point, they started to receive random volleys of Patriot musketry. The British troops had an extra incentive to get across as fast as possible; for they were unable to fire back while holding their weapons over their heads.[25] Before leaving the opposite banks, they had tied their leather cartridge boxes around their necks to protect the powder. In an act of great courage and panache, Lord Cornwallis had plunged headlong into the Catawba with these first troops, and he would be one of the first to reach land on the opposite bank riding a fatally wounded mount. It is only at this point in which Lieutenant Davidson's picket started to flee.[26]

Within several minutes young Robert Henry saw the British force collect themselves, load their weapons, and lower their muskets in preparation for firing a volley at the fleeing men. The volley echoed in the woods and missed Henry who had taken shelter behind a tree, but one round struck and mortally injured his former schoolmaster Robert Beatty in the hip. He pleaded for Henry to make haste: "It's time to run, Bob"[27] The boy did this with great speed and ran right past mounted reinforcements and General Davidson, who had yet to see that the British had actually landed in force on the shore. Joseph Graham, who was reportedly with the Patriot cavalry, noted that " ...by the time they {the militia cavalry} got there, tied their horses, and came up in line to the high bank above the ford in front of the column, it was within fifty yards of the eastern shore."[28]

General Davidson, having approached the shoreline quickly, realized that he was too late with his reinforcements to catch the British in the river; he then ordered that the cavalry should reform some two hundred yards to the rear in case the British had mounted troops already across. Davidson then ordered Colonel Polk's Mecklenburg militia to support what was left of the picket.

Men were still fleeing into the woods as Col. Polk shouted: 'Fire away boys; there is help at hand" and then turned in his saddle to give further orders to his men. It was at this point, during what had to be a cacophony of sounds and shouts, that he noticed General Davidson gazing at a solitary figure on the shore holding a gun with a barrel still smoldering from a recent shot.[29] Without a word, the general collapsed from his mount, obviously dead. No attempt was made by those who saw the General fall to reclaim his body due to the proximity of the approaching British troops. Oral tradition still holds that it was the Tory guide who recognized the general and had fired the fatal shot.

To add to this tragedy, General Davidson's last daring efforts had been to persuade the militia to make a brave stand. Upon seeing Davidson's death, his troops melted into the woods. One must remember that many of the volunteers probably, in the confusion of the action, may have misunderstood some of the orders being shouted out in haste. Seeing that the British forces had arrived in force on the near bank, they perhaps determined that orders to regroup at the rally point had been issued. Some three hundred of the supposed eight hundred militia were to be found several hours after the engagement clogging the roads along with many other refugees; fleeing the approach of the enemy.

Torrence's Tavern or Tarrant's Tavern, a well-known landmark of the time located several miles north of Cowan's Ford on the path to Salisbury, had been selected as the central rallying point. With the roads ever filling with more and more of those fearing the British advance, Col. Tarleton and his Tory Legion saw their chance to incite terror on the local population. They pursued the fleeing patriots with wild shouts of revenge for Cowpens, burning and pillaging what ever they came across as they approached the Patriot rally point. Tradition holds that a general charge, with sabers flashing in the sun, occurred as they approached the tavern. Tarleton recorded some 50 killed and several hundred routed near the tavern.[30]

Regardless of the questionable placement of the militia, or actions of any individuals, the British undoubtedly suffered heavier casualties than the Patriots, though the figures have been debated over the years. Lord Cornwallis tried to downplay the loss and emphasized the bravery that his men presented in the face of the enemy: "Lord Cornwallis desires the Brigade of Guards will Accept his Warmest acknowledgements for the Cool & Determin'd Bravery which they shew'd at the Passage of the Catabau, when rushing through that long and Difficult Ford under a Galling fire without returning a Shot, give him a most pleasing prospect of what may be expected from that distinguished Corps...."[31] Cornwallis only reported four dead (including Colonel Hall) and more than thirty wounded.[32]

The numbers generally given are that the Patriot forces lost between four to twelve men (the latter number may be in addition to the losses following the action at Torrence's Tavern), whereas the British lost anywhere between fourteen to a hundred men. Bodies of the British and German soldiers floated down river and became entangled in the brush and in fishing traps.[33] Locals reported that they found many of the troopers had actually drowned rather than having lost their lives from being shot. For days after the battle, their carcasses filled the river with a horrid stench.[34]

General Davidson's body, which had been totally stripped, was located that evening by Major David Wilson, Rev. Thomas McCaule and Richard Barry.[35] Here too is a debate. While it is well known that the British did capture his wallet, which was more of a leather briefcase full of official papers and communications for intelligence, it is debated if they stripped him completely. Local legend has it that the British intentionally stripped the young general and even took time to desecrate the body, then leaving it where it lay on the muddy bank of the river. Naturally, this story could be American propaganda that dates back to the war itself.

In an act of bravery in its own right the General's widow, Mary Brevard Davidson, left her numerous children- including her one month-old child- and went through miles of enemy-held territory to be present at her husband's burial at Hopewell Presbyterian Church in northern Mecklenburg. General Davidson should have been buried at his home church, Center Presbyterian in Mount Mourne, yet by the time that his body was recovered, the area was decidedly under British control. The body of the general was placed in a donated blue suit, shrouded with a cloth, and was buried by torchlight while rain fell on the mourners.[36] His remains are still at Hopewell Presbyterian Church to this day.[37] A stately marker now adorns his tomb. Annually, the church and the Daughters of the American Revolution commemorate his courage. General Davidson may have been laid to rest, yet history was not finished with him or with the battle in which he lost his life.

Post-Mortem:
The Man and the Battle

The battle itself lasted less than an hour. Young General William Lee Davidson lost his life, and the local militia evaporated and was of no further assistance to General Greene. Lord Cornwallis, with great vigor, crossed the Catawba in force. How is it that many historical accounts over the years assert that this stand on the Catawba River was a great display of local patriotism, and was a resounding success? The answer to this question has many facets. One aspect that is not disputed is that General Davidson's death, or "martyrdom," would serve as the perfect symbol of Revolutionary courage and leadership for many future Carolinians during different resurgences of regional and national pride.

A researcher of this skirmish will first observe the event is much overlooked in major historical works. As already noted, the "battle" occurred between several larger and more noted engagements of the war, Kings Mountain, Cowpens and Guilford Courthouse. For a historian it is therefore still somewhat virgin territory. Very few well-known works have had more than a few paragraphs, or at most, a few narrative pages mentioning the engagement on the Catawba.[38] Thus, no one has taken an in-depth historiographical look at the different accounts of the battle or its impact. However, there have been several specific times in the past two centuries that there has been great public interest in recounting General Davidson's bold stand on the Catawba.

William Lee Davidson as a man, like the battle, is somewhat elusive as well. However, some absolutes one can ascertain. He was of Scotch-Irish heritage whose father, George Davidson, immigrated to America years before and the family eventually acquired a plot of land in the piedmont region. Being the middle son, he inherited a moderate tract of land near Fourth Creek upon his father's passing.[39] His two brothers fade from history, and little is known of them after the 1760s.[40]

According to several accounts, he had a natural education of a planter and was literate with somewhat of a formal education. It is debated whether his "proper education" was at an academy or through a private tutor. Regardless of the holes in the historical record of his upbringing, by the time of the American Revolution, he was an established man; well respected by his peers, his church, and the community. Davidson had even served in the Continental Army earlier at Germantown and Valley Forge along with General Washington. One can say that he was an experienced "combat veteran" by the time the British made their move towards the Catawba. In short, William Lee Davidson was worthy as any to command the troops that now faced Lord Cornwallis.

The first published accounts of the engagement on the Catawba were to be found in the memoirs of those who were there. Not surprisingly, the first on record is from one of the commanders, the famed (or infamous) Lieutenant-Colonel Banastre Tarleton. His memoir, entitled *History of the Campaigns of 1780 and 1781 in the Southern Provinces,* was first published in 1787. In it, much like Lord Cornwallis' comments from the *British Orderly Book,* Tarleton emphasized the bravery of the British forces, embellished the strength of the enemy, and altered the statistics inflicted by both sides to put the British in a better light: "As soon as the light company entered the water, supported by the grenadiers and the two battalions, the enemy commenced a galling and constant fire which was steadily received by the guards without being returned." He goes on to say, "The attack of the light and grenadier companies, as soon as they reached the land, dispersed the Americans, who left their leader General Davidson, dead upon the spot and about forty men killed and wounded. Lieutenant-Colonel Hall, of the light infantry, fell as he quit the stream. The guards had very few men killed, and only thirty-six wounded."[41]

Here again, one should notice the number of casualties. It matches Lord Cornwallis' count as reported. Tarleton may have even referred to the official record for his statistical information. Besides, it is known at this point in time that Tarleton wished to support his former commanding officer's account of the campaigns. However, Tarleton's views in the years that followed the war would change and his political relationship with Lord Cornwallis would gradually deteriorate.

In general, local accounts of the Battle of Cowan's Ford were simply passed down orally in the years following the war. Personal accounts would in time find their way into periodicals, memoirs, and correspondences. An example can be seen in a letter from Gen. Joseph Graham to Judge A. D. Murphey. Dated November 27th, 1820, Gen. Graham writes in hindsight: "Dear Sir... I will give you a kind chronology (of Revolutionary engagements in the Carolinas) according to my present views." The letter goes on to mention the meeting between the Patriot officers at Beattie's but not the engagement at Cowan's or the death of General Davidson.[42] Yet, later in his published papers (released in 1904), it would recount the battle and Davidson's death with great detail.[43]

Many accounts were drafted to paper for the first time in trying to verify service in the hopes of gaining a pension from the state. Thus, the 1820's through 1830's would be the first high-mark in the recollection and interest in the Battle of Cowan's Ford. This recounting of service for pension benefits played itself out all over the nation. As noted in Alfred F. Young's work *The Shoemaker and the Tea Party*, "The angry voices of veterans eventually achieved a new pension act in 1832 eliminating the means test and requiring only 'a full account of service,' which, much to the surprise of the politicians, led to another twenty thousand applications."[44]

Another noteworthy account, as already mentioned, was that of militia volunteer Robert Henry. Henry survived the war and lived to within several weeks of celebrating his 98th birthday, dying in February of 1863.[45] During his long life, Henry had become a well respected surveyor, teacher and lawyer. Before his death, Henry wrote down his recollections of his military service during the Revolutionary War. His son William L. Henry sent the original manuscripts to his good friend Dr. J. F. E. Hardy in Ashville, North Carolina. Henry's account was subsequently first published in 1891 at the behest of Dr. J.F.E. Hardy. It stands as a rare first-hand account of the battle as it unfolded from the eyes of a 16-year-old volunteer.[46]

One can also tell that his account was written down after the publication of John H. Wheeler's work, *History of North Carolina* or (*Historical Sketches of North Carolina: From 1584 to 1851, Compiled From Original Records, Official Documents and Traditional Statement ; With Biographical sketches of her distinguished Statesmen, Jurists, Lawyers, Soldiers, Divines, Etc.*) published in 1851. For Henry takes issue with how certain events occurred according to Wheeler's work. Henry asserts that Wheeler's statistics of killed and injured due to the Patriot's volleys were inaccurate, and that Davidson's total militia force probably only number three hundred rather than the six to eight hundred as noted in other works.[47] This may be due to his arrival at the ford after the disbursement of the other troops to their assigned stations. It is probably historically safe to claim that General Davidson did have around eight hundred troops prior to dispersal. General Morgan specifically remarked this to Greene on January 29th in a communiqué.[48] Being that every man was important, one doubts that Morgan would have exaggerated given the circumstances.

Another assertion from Henry's narrative is that Gen. Joseph Graham, whom he was acquainted with, was not there during the initial part of the engagement.[49] Henry takes time to refute Wheeler's use of Graham's account which portrays his recollection of the fight as very historically accurate and significant.

Henry does, however, support other accounts that Gen. Davidson had established his main camp some distance (three-fourths of a mile) away from Ford. It was even remarked to Henry, by a junior officer at the camp, that it seemed that Davidson was ill-posted for the impending attack. Yet, it is likely that this junior officer was not privy to the knowledge that Col. Tarleton might attempt a cavalry screen prior to the crossing.[50]

One of the most interesting parts of Henry's narrative is that it lists by name local Tories that took part in the battle on the behalf of the British. Henry mentions the "British pilot" Dick Beal, a man who knew the area well, as being the one who led the British during the dark hours to the ford. Henry also noted that even though Dick Beal was initially fooled by some of the diversionary campfires, it was Beal who felled Gen. Davidson with a fatal shot soon after the lead British and German elements had reached the far banks.[51] However, others place the British Tory "pilot" as one Frederick Hager or (Hagar) which guided Cornwallis during the crossing and killed Gen. Davidson. The truth will probably never be known with any certainty.[52] Interestingly, in one published roll of American Loyalists, a Frederick Hager joined Colonel Samuel Campbell's North Carolina Regimental Militia in Charleston, South Carolina. The registry lists the enlistment from May 6th, 1782 to August 5th, 1782. [53] This enlistment is certainly after the engagement on the Catawba, but lends itself to a member of the Hager family being a Tory.

Henry's narrative supports that much of the militia withdrew into the woods as Davidson approached to assess the situation. After a personal heroic stand, he and the injured schoolmaster Beatty retreated in the face of greater numbers. Henry successfully made his way back towards friendly territory, and eventually returned his borrowed weapon to his brother.

After the engagement, he then tabulated around seven volleys that he had loosed at the British, including at least one fatally striking a redcoat by his reckoning.[54] It was truly a memorable experience for a patriotic teen of the time.

Davidson College, the Presbytery and Lasting Legacies.

At the same time that the elderly veterans were trying to gain their much deserved pensions from the state, the Presbytery of Concord proposed buying land for the expressed purpose of establishing a school. It is noted in the Concord Presbytery Records of 1832-1836: "The committee appointed at the last meeting of Presbytery to purchase Lands and appoint agents to collect funds for the Manual Labor School reported and their report was accepted and is as follows: viz. Agreeably to appointment the Committee met on the 13th of May 1835 at the House of Wm. Davidson, Esq., in Mecklenburg County...."[55]

The William Davidson mentioned in this record is the son, the one-month old child, that Mary Brevard Davidson left behind on that sad, rain-drenched night in 1781 to attend her husband's funeral. William Davidson (junior) had matured and had become a well known and respected member of the Mecklenburg community. He would also donate, on behalf of the family, several hundred acres to what would become the college that would proudly bear their name. Ironically, he too was seeking a pension. William and his siblings had a right to petition for a pension, being at the time of their father's death they were children, and their father had served seven years as a Lieutenant-Colonel in the Continental Line. This petition was granted and is noted in the North Carolina State Records, volume XXII. [56]

It was no coincidence that the Presbytery met in the Davidson house; it had already been discussed what the envisioned institution should be called: "A proposition being offered that the Institution be named. It was resolved that the Manual Labor Institution which we are about to build be called Davidson College a tribute to the memory of that distinguished and excellent man Gen. Wm Davidson who in the ardor of patriotism, fearlessly contending for the Liberty of his country fell (universally lamented) in the Battle of Cowan's Ford."[57]

On August 2nd, 1838 a small crowd gathered in the sweltering heat to hear the opening invocation speech of Davidson College's first president, Rev. Robert Hall Morrison. Typical of the nineteenth century, the speech is lengthy and traces the roots of western academia from the Greeks forward, thus lasting an agonizing two hours. In his concluding remarks the Rev. Morrison stated, "In the advancement of such a work we are permitted to meet together today and to mingle our congratulations and our prayers. The want of patriotic veneration shown by the legislative councils of our country for the name of a distinguished General, who fell on the 1st of February, 1781, six miles from this place, has permitted the patrons of this college to connect his name with its destiny, and to hope for a more imperishable memorial to his worth, than the cold and silent pillars of a common monument could give."[58]

Also speaking at this event was the first faculty member, a Professor P.S. Sparrow. Fortunately for the crowd, his speech only lasted around twenty minutes. Sparrow did not give reference to the famed general, but he did touch on the heart of what the Presbytery was trying to achieve in the 1830's: "Well, my hearers, if such is your determination (to build an institution), it is proper to remind you, that it will require much prayer, and labor, and money; but it will be prayer, and labor, and money expended in a good cause. You can form but a very imperfect idea of the magnitude of the enterprise in which you are engaged." Sparrow then struck at the heart of an idea, "What could the founders of Princeton College if they could rise from their graves, and behold all that has been achieved by their Institution? What would be your sensations if you could see the history of Davidson College, in perspective, for a hundred years to come?"[59]

What could be more revealing of the college founders, investors, the Presbytery, and leading citizens of the Mecklenburg had in the late 1830's about the envisioned future? It is clear that they were establishing the primacy of the region, not only using the name of a legendary local Revolutionary War hero for their private school, but at the same time also emphasizing that the Mecklenburg region (with its institutions) could in time become the center for education, economic growth, and progress in North Carolina.

Townships were growing in the state during the mid-1830's. As Hugh Lefler and Ray Newsome mentioned in their work *History of a Southern State: North Carolina*, "The expanding economic life of the state after 1835 was reflected in an increase in the number and size of towns."[60] Even Davidson College was seeing a rise in enrollment during this time according to Thomas H. Hamilton, a student in 1837: "We had about 64 students this session and there are some more coming in a few weeks that we know of and doubtless some others that we know not of...."[61] Many of the Presbytery leaders had attended Princeton, and one does not have to wonder if their experiences of a classical education in a growing and prosperous New Jersey had left a lasting impression on them. It also stands to reason that if New England, as a whole, was "rediscovering" the Revolution in the mid-1830's, this conservative elite of North Carolina would follow the example by laying claim to its own local martyr.

During the second-half of the nineteenth century, the Battle of Cowan's Ford was recounted in much the same patriotic light: a valiant stand for liberty. School texts in North Carolina in the 1880's noted, "This was attempted (British chasing Morgan by crossing the Catawba) at Cowan's

Ford, and the British, after some loss, forced a passage. Unfortunately, brave General Davidson, who was in command of the militia, was killed...."[62] In Cornelia Spencer's *First Steps in North Carolina History,* just a line is given to the event, "In the skirmish here (Cowan's Ford) about twenty of our patriots were killed, and among them was the noble and intrepid General Davidson...."[63] In other words, not much was said of the engagement.[64]

The 1920's, however, experienced a great surge of interest in General Davidson and the Battle of Cowan's Ford. In 1920, the Mecklenburg Chapter of the Daughters of the American Revolution raised money and erected an ornate monument at General Davidson's grave at Hopewell Presbyterian Church. As recorded in the college's paper *The Davidsonian*: "On the evening of September 29th, (1920) at Hopewell Church, eleven miles from Charlotte on the Beatty's Ford road, a large gathering attended the impressive ceremonies at the dedication of a beautiful bronze memorial tablet erected to the memory of Gen. William Lee Davidson, by the Mecklenburg Chapter of the American Daughters of the Revolution or DAR. Up to this time the grave has been unmarked, and the movement to suitably honor the memory of General Davidson was started by the Mecklenburg Declaration of Independence Chapter."[65]

In 1948, a chapter of the DAR located in Nashville, Tennessee would form in honor of the late general. To this day the General William Lee Davidson Chapter of the DAR is still active in the preservation, and continued education, of our nation's heritage. Their connection to the general is that in 1783 his family relocated to a plot of land granted to them, some 5,750 acres, in what is now Davidson County, Tennessee. General Davidson's proud legacy now spans two states.[66]

The General and the "Mecklenburg Declaration"

The *Charlotte Observer* has published many articles on the battle over the years, General Davidson, and another interesting claim to Revolutionary fame, the Mecklenburg Declaration of Independence. Since the 1820's, there has been a claim that Mecklenburg County had claimed its independence from the British Empire months before the well-known Philadelphia Declaration of Independence of 1776. It is known, and understood, that there were some "resolves" made much like many other colonies at the time. But a full-blown break with England is very questionable. Certainly if this claim could be substantiated, it would not only change many of the history texts, but also gain some measure national recognition for the Charlotte-Mecklenburg region. The argument over the authenticity has been reheated since the turn of the century.

Richard N. Current wrote in his article titled: *"That Other Declaration: May 20, 1775- May 20, 1975,"* that North Carolina was somewhat ridiculed by other well-known states that could claim a colorful historical tie to the Revolution. Current recounts the event that started the argument: "When in 1819, the question came up in Congress, men from Massachusetts disputed the Virginia claim (that Virginia had led the way to the Revolution). And then a North Carolinian stepped forth to assert that neither Massachusetts nor Virginia had started the movement for independence. No indeed; the honor rightfully belonged to North Carolina."[67]

Members in Congress naturally objected and scoffed at the idea. Current adds that, "So the long-serving senator from North Carolina,

Nathaniel Macon, and the freshman representative from the Mecklenburg district, William Davidson wrote home for documentary proof." [68] To make a long story short, the original manuscript, left by a signer John McKnitt Alexander, had been destroyed in a house fire in 1800. No old publications, copies or other records of the May 20th Declaration could be located, and only a small group of elderly men could be found to give eyewitness testimony which did not always corroborate each other.[69] Many North Carolina advocates attempted to find irrefutable proof of the Mecklenburg Declaration over the next century to no avail.

The regional press ran successive articles in late twenties connecting the supposed Mecklenburg Declaration with the slightly dramatized accounts of the Revolutionary War in the South. Typical is this excerpt from an August 7th, 1927 article: "The signing of the Mecklenburg Declaration of Independence, over which a controversy has taken place since about the year 1820, and which most historians agree upon as an actual historical event, although some claim the date was May 31 instead of May 20 while other hold that there were two distinct events, the signing of the declaration on May 20 and the promulgating of a set of resolves on May 31, is the most memorable happening in this section in the year 1775."[70]

On the second full page of war-chronology in this article, our hero Davidson is portrayed with great courage along with the "gallant" Mecklenburg Militia: "As the Americans were busily defending the slopes (over the horse ford) of the oncoming British, General Davidson was shot and fell. The spot where he stood at the time the fatal bullet struck him is known and pointed out to those who like to ramble over the historic scene. General Davidson was bravely directing his men and it is said that he was dashing up and down along his line when he was hit. He fell from his horse and several of his men carried him back to a small house."[71]

In a 1931 *Charlotte Observer* article entitled "Sent Her Scotch-Irish Sons To Trace Out New Frontiers," many of the well-established families in the Charlotte area were mentioned as true American frontiersmen. Yet the only three sections that were headed in bold print on the first page was "Death of Davidson," "Story about Jackson" and the "Mecklenburg Declaration."[72] General Davidson's name peppers the entire article, even in the introductory section it states, "...it was a Mecklenburg patriot who met his (Cornwallis's) army at Cowan's Ford on the Catawba and gave his life to repel the foreign foe...."[73]

In the section dedicated just to General Davidson, patriotism finds expression in one of the two poems written about the death of the General. Historic liberties were obviously taken to stir the American spirit:

We buried him darkly at dead of night,
The sod with our bayonets turning, by the struggling moonbeam's misty light,
And the lantern dimly burning.
No useless coffin enclosed his breast,
Not in sheet or in shroud we wound him, but he lay like a warrior taking his rest,
With his martial cloak around him.
Few and short were the prayers we said, and we spoke not a word of sorrow,
But we steadfastly gazed on the face of the dead,
And we bitterly thought of the morrow.
Slowly and sadly we laid him down, from the field of his fame fresh and gory,
We carved not a line and we raised not a stone,
But we left him alone with his glory.[74]

Continuing on, one eventually comes to the "Mecklenburg Declaration" section in which it is boldly stated: "Looking backward from effect to cause one of the strongest reasons, manifest, for the acceptance of the fact of the Mecklenburg Declaration of Independence, is the type of people who came out of Mecklenburg, their characteristics, as evident in their history, and the stock which logically would breed such frontiersmen."[75] Media sensationalism can run rampant in any historical era, and the next two full pages of type-print that follows, which included the various headings: "William Davidson," "Stealing a Chicken," "A Joint Reunion," and "Virtues of Ancestry." The conclusion that one can draw from this is obvious: General Davidson had become a symbol, a spokesman if you will, for Charlotte-Mecklenburg and its inheritance from the Revolution.

One might consider that this was just local ballyhoo, and would gain little national attention. However, the initial spark in the growth of Revolutionary interest may have been caused by a national figure. President Woodrow Wilson visited the Charlotte area in May of 1916. As recounted in former Davidson College President Walter Lee Lingle's *Memories of Davidson College*, "President Woodrow Wilson paid an unexpected visit to Davidson College on May 20th, 1916. He came to Charlotte to take part in the celebration of the one hundred and forty-first anniversary of the Mecklenburg Declaration of Independence."[76] Wilson was careful, and made only indirect references to the mysterious Mecklenburg Declaration. One must remember that President Wilson was in a precarious spot, being a historian himself, and yet a Presbyterian and a former Davidson College student. It then is not hard to see that in the wake of an American victory in World War I, and the economic boom and prosperity of the early twenties, why Charlotte might wish to again boast of its Revolutionary claims to fame.

In 1951 Dr. Chalmers G. Davidson, yet another relative of the late General, published the first and only full biography on General Davidson which is entitled the *"Piedmont Partisan: The Life and Times of Brigadier-General William Lee Davidson."* Dr. Davidson, who was the school's archivist at the time, traced in his work the Scotch Calvinists migration to the Carolinas, the Presbyterians dealings with the Revolutionary Congress, and the life and death of North Carolina's most famed General at Cowan's Ford. Dr. Davidson generally supported Mecklenburg's claim to independence, and places General Davidson in an interesting position: "Although frequently given the credit, William Davidson does not appear to have been a member of the Mecklenburg Independence Committee of Safety. He did, however, see a copy of the transactions adopted in Charlotte before it was sent to Congress, and gave the sentiments his hearty endorsement."[77] Interestingly, Dr. Davidson gave little reference as to how he could support this historical information.[78] One can, on the other hand, see that he did challenge long-held beliefs that the General was actually on the committee that composed the questionable document, yet Dr. Davidson placed his famous relative in the position of having seen and supported the famed document.

One could say that Dr. Davidson "played it safe." Knowing his local audience and supporters, he was able to remove General Davidson "historically" from the Mecklenburg committees, yet at the same time he was compelled to place him in a supportive role. Dr. Davidson takes this cautious stand throughout the work right up to a final assessment of the General himself. He makes several assertions that may have shocked a few readers during this revival of patriotic zeal; Dr. Davidson dared to criticize the General's military stature.

Dr. Davidson exclaimed that the General was called to do his duty, and was not a charismatic and spontaneous personality: "Unlike Andrew Jackson, who as a lad may well have run errands for the Brigadier at Waxhaw, Davidson was not of the dynamic and explosive strain of Scotch-Irishman who would foment a revolution if none existed."[79] He then admits that Cowan's Ford was an overall strategic defeat for the Patriots, but places General Davidson in an important light: "What he (Greene) did not know was the extent to which Davidson's personality controlled the Salisbury militia. Hundreds responded to the backwoods Brigadier who would hear no other voice."[80] Thus pointing out that with William Lee Davidson dead, militia volunteers in the Carolinas would dwindle to a trickle and offer little further support to the "Patriot Cause."[81]

In the closing chapters of the work, Dr. Davidson stresses the widely held view that the General was loyal, trustworthy, precise in his orders, resourceful, and charming to those that knew him; a man of true iconic American virtues. In other words, General Davidson possessed qualities that any group of regional conservatives would be proud to claim as their own.[82]

A decade after *Piedmont Partisan*, another noted local work was published called *Hornets' Nest*. In it, General Davidson is portrayed again as a resourceful local leader. However, the General is not directly associated with the Mecklenburg Declaration of Independence. Like the *Piedmont Partisan,*, his "Mecklenburg character" is an underlying theme throughout the narrative.

The publication of the *Hornets' Nest* occurred when the Charlotte-Mecklenburg area was again seeing economic growth of the 1950s and 1960s. A new hydroelectric dam was just being completed at, of all places, Cowan's Ford when this work was written. The authors, LeGette Blythe and Charles Brockmann, both claimed ancestry to signers of the Mecklenburg Declaration of Independence (one claiming family links to General Davidson).[83] LeGette Blythe, it should be noted, was one of the columnists for the *Charlotte Observer* in 1927 that discussed, at length, both General Davidson and the Mecklenburg Declaration.[84]

Not much had changed since the twenties. Blythe's stand on the issues remained the same: "Mecklenburg does have a dramatic story. And through the years the county has had the good fortune to have had her story recorded in published volumes. Even more fortunately, numerous documents contemporary with the making of history have survived to authenticate the accounts related by the historians."[85] This was in direct reference to the preceding paragraph that stated 'One needs no further proof of the authenticity of the Mecklenburg Declaration of Independence than to live a few years in this country.'[86] As time rolled forward into the Bicentennial Era, works such as the *Hornets' Nest* and *Piedmont Partisan* were taken as pure historic gospel by the local press and much of the general population.

When one looks across history, one realizes how timing plays a major factor, sometimes very fortuitously. In 1970, a bulldozer operator was bulldozing back brush and small trees near the McGuire Nuclear Station when it ran across an ivy-covered eight-foot pile of river-stones. This pile of stones turned out to be an archaic monument erected by a relative of the General, one E.L. Baxter Davidson, probably in the late 1920s, to commemorate his famous relative's role in the Battle of Cowan's Ford.[87] The finding of this monument at the dawn of the Bicentennial could not have been better timed.

Interest in the monument was immediate; newspapers around the area soon reported of public interest in commemorating its ties with the past. On February 1st, 1971, exactly one-hundred ninety years after the battle, a new and larger monument was dedicated. A large plaque tells of the engagement, and even has a small relief depiction of General Davidson's final moments. The area was landscaped and the old monument was moved near the new monument that now overlooks the highway that runs past the nuclear power station.

Present at the dedication were representatives of Duke Power, the Mecklenburg Historical Association, and Dr. Chalmers Davidson, who was naturally asked to speak.[88] Surprisingly, this was not the only monument to North Carolina's most noted general. A joint resolution of Congress in 1903 appropriated funds to erect a monument; only this monument was not erected at the battle site. It was, however, placed on the grounds of the Guilford Courthouse Battlegrounds. Congress had, in times past, attempted to appropriate funds for a monuments (1781, 1821, 1841, and 1842), but public funds were scarce, and few monuments were ever constructed.[89] Even through private funding, one might expect to see a modest bronze figure of General Davidson mounted on a charger in the commons area of the college campus. In fact to this day, Davidson College surprisingly has no such monument to its namesake on campus grounds as might be seen on other major well-established institutions.

All through the seventies, especially 1975 and 1976, news articles appeared recounting the Battle of Cowan's Ford. *The Tar Heel Spotlight* on January 30th, 1975 ran an article entitled "Davidson Lost the Battle, But American Won the War." The *Statesville Record & Landmark* in its Bicentennial edition ran a multi-page layout with the leading section "Battle With British At Catawba River Takes Life of Gen. Davidson." Even in the state capital, *The News and Observer* in Raleigh ran on February 8th, 1976 "Minor Battle on Catawba Took Life of N.C. Leader." All of these articles sang the same patriotic lyrics, many citing Dr. Chalmers Davidson's work and memoir accounts like *Gen. Joseph Graham and his Revolutionary Papers*. There can be no question that General Davidson's legacy had evolved, by the late nineteen-seventies, into North Carolina's preeminent "Revolutionary Icon," not just Charlotte-Mecklenburg's.

Interest still continues to this day. The late Reverend Jeff Lowrance, former pastor of Hopewell Presbyterian Church and avid local historian, was able to temporarily gain access to the Davidson wallet in 2001. A representative from the British Public Records Office in London, where the wallet had been kept since the Revolutionary War, accompanied it under tight security to a public showing at the Davidson Town Hall on July 3rd, 2001.[90] Undoubtedly, local interest exists in the General and the battle in which he lost his life.

In final analysis, how should one view General William Lee Davidson and his fateful stand on the Catawba? Certainly he was brave and daring, and as Dr. Chalmers Davidson stresses, his true importance was in gaining militia support in the backcountry of the Carolinas. After General Davidson's death, no other person seemed to possess the persuasiveness, respect, and good report with the regional rebels.

However, some might disagree with Dr. Davidson's assessment that given his short time directly commanding troops in action, "Perhaps he (General Davidson) was a brilliant strategist. He was never given a chance to prove it."[91] This rearguard action was a fitting test of his military leadership, having shown that there is factual room for argument in regards to Davidson's deployment of troops, and the impact that it could have had on Lord Cornwallis' forces. Here again, despite John Shy's statement on the "Napoleonic Standard" that many armchair military historians often use, one cannot be completely conclusive on assessing General Davidson's overall tactics and strategy. Certainly given the historic evidence, he faced a truly daunting task and did his best.

If there is one absolute that can be drawn from this historical event, it is that Davidson's untimely death gave North Carolina, and particularly the Charlotte-Mecklenburg region, a local martyr as a direct link to the Revolutionary past. General Davidson has served in this capacity very well. His name will still be used, as in the past, as the region's changing historical needs require. Alfred F. Young validates this point in his work, *The Shoemaker and the Tea Party*. In reference to the "Boston Tea Party," Young remarked that "Indeed, the best sign that the Tea Party has become a national icon is that it is claimed by people at so many points on the American political spectrum."[92] Similarly, General William Lee Davidson is still faithfully serving his country and community when the duty to historic memory calls.

Something similar might be said about the Battle of Cowan's Ford. Though its legacy has been mostly claimed by a group of elite conservatives in the Charlotte-Mecklenburg region during most of the nineteenth and early twentieth centuries, by the latter part of the twentieth century, one can clearly see that Cowan's Ford had evolved to represent more than just a small group. Many native Carolinians have come to claim a connection with the battle and those who fought in it. One comes to realize that much of the Carolina's "public memory" of the Revolutionary War has been shaped by the death of a courageous thirty-four-year-old general during a desperate skirmish on a cold rain-soaked day in February, 1781.

A Poem-

"His {Davidson's} riderless charger returned form the battle,

A gallant, a beautiful, valiant black steed;

The saddle so empty, the trappings, the rattle

Were tidings enough in those times of dread need.

He died for his country beside his own river

He mingled his blood with its onrushing tied,

He died as a hero- he knew not a quiver-

An American patriot, he lived as he died."

An excerpt from "Cowan's Ford"
by: Maude Waddell, Charleston, S.C.
Circa, 1931.

Gen. Davidson's Grave at Hopewell Presbyterian Church

Changing Times
and Future Possibilities

In the last thirty years, the region around the Catawba River and its manmade Lake Norman has changed greatly. I grew up around the lake area and remember a time when a man could grab a rifle and legally go hunting within walking distance of his home. Many of the people whom I knew growing up had surnames that could be seen gracing the headstones of the oldest local cemeteries. Rarely did a person run across someone whose family had not been established in the area for over a century. Yet, with the development of the region, and its newly found affluence during the late 1970s and 1980s, many of the old families have either moved away or faded into the deluge of newcomers. With this growth, many of the old landmarks of the area have changed as well.

No one, especially in this time of recession, is complaining about the economic benefits of businesses like NASCAR, banking, and tourism bring to the area. However, there is a price that is being paid for such growth. Many people who have moved into the Mecklenburg, Catawba, and Iredell regions have no real knowledge of its historical past. The good news is that many of these newcomers to the region are starting to take an interest in local history. As a history teacher at a local high school, I have met the parents of many students. More than once I found my discussion with them wander from their student's grade to some local event of the past. Historic commissions and committees are seemingly springing up all of the time. Even so, the unabated development that has occurred during this intermediate time has had an impact on historical locations.

Cowan's Ford, to some varying degree, is still there. A bridge now spans the chasm that separates the two banks of the Catawba near where the British crossing occurred. In the 1960s Duke Energy built a dam for its power station along the Catawba. The station and the dam now border the old ford area. Besides these modern intrusions, the river and the surrounding actual engagement area are still much as it would have appeared two centuries ago. In fact, due to the plant's proximity to the ford, it may have prevented further development along this very section of the river. Unfortunately, due to another attack on our liberty and safety on September 11th, 2001 access to the crossing area at Cowan's Ford is restricted because of the power plant's new security protocols. Another loss is that the actual fords of Beattie's and Sherrald's (Sherrill's) are now lost under the ever popular lake. However, roads and localities still bear their name.

Within several hundred yards of the bridge, the "General Davidson Monument" can be seen. Unfortunately, like many monuments, the Davidson Monument (or should I say monuments as the early 20th century monument is still there as well) is being reclaimed by nature and falling victim to virtual abandonment. In December of 2009, I went back to the monument and Cowan's Ford after not seeing it since I was in junior high during the early 1980s. A generation ago, it was well maintained with flowers around the base of the large brick monument, and a full-sized cannon proudly stood in defiance of British tyranny.

In 2009 I was amazed to find that the cannon had been removed, and trash was strewn over the entire area. The monuments themselves were hard to see from the road as the trees have grown in the last twenty years. Just over the tree line, behind the monuments, a modern industrial building can be seen. There were, much to my surprise, two pickups in the monument parking lot when I pulled in; but these men were meeting there just to exchange a sofa. I pointed out the monument to them, and they looked at me as if I was from Mars.

Other monuments or places of historical importance see similar fates across our nation. This goes back to public interest or lack thereof. The rock on which Cornwallis' men camped near Mount Mourne is now hidden by a medical office, and a new off ramp (Langtree Road, Exit 31) on Interstate 77 connects with the very road that the British cavalry under the "Green Dragoon" Banastre Tarleton charged down to assault the fleeing militia at Torrence's Tavern. The small DAR monument that marks this event is almost hidden from sight unless one knows exactly where to look. Further up the road in Statesville, North Carolina, a French and Indian War Fort (Fort Dobbs) has been a historic site for many years but not utilized to its full capacity. Mounds of unrecognizable dirt trenches and a small shack are about all that is currently there, though there are plans to possibly rebuild the fort (given funding) in the near future.

It must be remembered at this point that many communities owe a great debt of gratitude to groups like the Daughters of the American Revolution, and similarly the Daughters of the Confederacy, to have taken the initiative in the past to mark sites and bring back social awareness to our nation's historic past. Without civic conscientious organizations such as these, which now have chapters that span much of the country, one wonders what else would have been lost in the name of "progress?"

A great opportunity to reclaim our historical past exists. In the same patriotic spirit of the 1820s and 1920s, our region at the turn of the new century has not only the chance to preserve these historic sites, but also gain economically from it. With the increase in traffic along the interstates that now cross the region, there is a chance to utilize our unique historic assets. The old maxim "killing two birds with one stone" comes to mind.

The one sure way to protect a historic site is for people to know of its existence and importance. Being that many of these regional sites are within a short drive off of a main thoroughfare (Interstate 77), it would be, as Thomas Paine might say, "common sense" that certain historic groups in conjunction with local business leaders might seize the opportunity to save, refurbish, and generally promote historic sites that are literally "right down the road."

Many visitors going across the region, especially families, on their way "to or fro" along the interstate might like to experience where part of our nation's history took place. The possibilities are there for those who have the foresight. Yet again, it is up to the people of this nation, and specifically this region of North Carolina, to decide the fate of many of these important historical sites before progress swallows them up. One must remember that, like the Battle of Cowan's Ford, history can be decided by a few dedicated and brave volunteers.

Chronology of Selected Events

1740s The Davidson family leaves Ireland for the American colonies.

May 20th   1775   The Mecklenburg Declaration?

July 4th   1776   The Declaration of Independence: Philadelphia, Pennsylvania.

May 12th   1780   British capture Charleston, South Carolina after a siege.

June 20th   1780   American Loyalist and Whig forces engage at Ramsour's Mill, (near present Lincolnton, North Carolina). Patriot victory.

August 16th   1780   British victory at the Battle of Camden, South Carolina.

October 7th   1780   Major Patriot victory at Kings Mountain, North/ South Carolina border area.

December 2nd 1780   General Nathaniel Greene takes command of the Southern army in Charlotte, North Carolina.

January 17th   1781   Patriot victory at the Battle of Cowpens (South Carolina) led by General Daniel Morgan. The victory is noted as a major shift in the tempo of the war in the South.

January 31st   1781   General Greene, Colonel William Washington, General Morgan, and General William Lee Davidson confers at Beattie's Ford. British reconnaissance arrives on the opposite bank during the discussion.

February 1st   1781 * Cornwallis crosses the Catawba River at Cowan's Ford. General William Lee Davidson and local militia contest his early morning crossing. General Davidson is killed leading his men.

February 1st   1781 * British chase and engage fleeing patriot militia at Torrence's Tavern near present day Mount Mourne and Mooresville, North Carolina.

March 15th   1781   Heated engagement between General Greene and Lord Cornwallis at Guilford Court House, North Carolina. Considered a British victory, but at a terrible cost in men and equipment.

October 19th   1781   Lord Cornwallis surrenders at Yorktown, Virginia.

September 3rd   1783   The Treaty of Paris (1783) British recognition of the United States as a separate nation.

1820s Increased applications for pensions due to military service during the American Revolutionary War.(First major revival of interest)

1837 Davidson College is founded.

1951 Publication of : *Piedmont Partisan; The Life and Times of Brigadier-General William Lee Davidson.* By Dr. Chalmers Davidson.

1963 Cowan's Ford Dam completed near the original battle site.

1960s- Current: Development of the Catawba and Lake Norman region.

Photographs

A view overlooking the general crossing area.

Cowan's Ford State Marker

Gen. Davidson's State Marker at Hopewell Church

Torrence's Tavern State Marker

DAR Torrence's Tavern Marker (early 20th century)

The Old Davidson Monument (early 20th Century)

The New Davidson Monument (1970s)

Robert Henry's Grave: Courtesy of Albert Spurr

Selected Transcriptions of Original Personal Notes and Communications of General William Lee Davidson

Along with small scraps of paper, and several pieces of North Carolina currency, these were correspondences reportedly within Davidson's wallet upon capture by the British, after General Davidson's death. Several text extracts from the minutes of Congress regulations governing the regular army of the United States from January 1, 1781 were also in his possession. The originals remain in the British Archives.

I. Communication on a scrap from a spy (unnamed) which listed figures and units known to be serving with Lord Cornwallis. Intelligence possibly gathered while the British were encamped at Ramsour's Mill :

3rd (Regiment of Foot)	700
Hessians	300
Yagers	100
23rd (Regiment of Foot)	300
33rd (Regiment of Foot)	300
M.V.	200
71st (Regiment of Foot)	200
Tarleton	200
	————
	2300

II. A scribbled scrap noting issuing of supplies/provisions:

67 rations between Dec. 5 - Jan. 15

III. A personal letter from a local widow to the general:

Sir,

I am the unfortunate women that is wife or other(wise) wife widow to Jas Whitlock who went with Colonel Brians. I have eight children to provide for and am at present in a condition very unable (mutilated for that or to ride to you in order to lay my case before you. A great deal of my property has been taken fro the use of the public or under that pretence but there is a negro boy of mine at Mr. Fortunes not returned to any commissioner that might help me greatly that I be returned at least for some time. And also there is 20 bushels of corn demanded of me for the use of the public which if taken will distress.

Yours
Sylvias Whitlock

Duchmancreek Jan. 20th, 1781
On reverse: H.E. William Davidson B.G.

IV. Form of enlistment into a regiment of North Carolina troops:

I do voluntarily enlist myself a private soldier in the first Regiment of North Carolina Continental forces commanded by Col Clark To serve for and during the sum of one year & an half and I do Acknowledge that I have no claim of bounty or reward for my service as a soldier except sufficient clothing and monthly pay as is or may be allowed to soldiers in the service of the United State of America.

(Signatures or marks of those enlisting)

V. General Davidson received a letter from William Sharpe. However, the core of the letter has been lost to history except for this extensive postscript:

Nov. 9 (1780)

P.S.

I forgot to inform (you) that Genl. Lincoln with upwards of an Hundred officers are lately exchanged and that the Commanders in Chief are about to negotiate a general exchange, including the convention troops and our militia. Gen. Washington is instructed to obtain a condition, that, the convention and other British prisoners shall not take the field nor bear arms before the first of May.

However humanity dictated an immediate exchange yet our present critical situation to the southward made it a great question in policy; was the exchange to take place immediately; and the enemy at liberty to arm and send forth their liberated troops it might be a fatal stroke to the state of North Carolina because in that state we have not arms stores & at present to put into the hands of our liberated troops & militia in order to make a vigorous defense. Therefore the delegates of North Carolina have been the means of keeping back the exchange a few weeks past and of qualifying the measure above mentioned with a view to get Gen. Greene in command- get forward some arms stores & and to get time to draw out and organize a little army, that may promise us some defense all wich I hope will sufficiently justify our conduct to our brave and virtuous officers and soldiers, who are in a distressing captivity. We have been so opposed in the business of delaying the exchange, by some of our neighboring delegates, who have a passionate fondness for their friends, that we have been threatened with the displeasure of those in captivity. These things have but little effect on the minds of men determined to do what appears to be right. I We (sic) are so well assured of the patriotism of our officers & soldiers, that they would at the risk of their lives endure six months of perhaps twenty months longer confinement rather than obtain liberty at the risk of a whole state.

Wm. Sharpe

On reverse: Genl. Davidson

VI. Another interesting communication within the British Archive is this letter dated one day prior to the engagement at Cowan's Ford. General Greene describes the general situation, and his amazement that more volunteers have not turned out to oppose the British advance in spite of General Davidson's constant requests.

Camp at Beatty's Ford
Jan. 31, 1781

Sir,

The enemy are laying on the opposite side of the river and from Every appearance seem determined to penetrate this country. Genl. Davidson informs he has called again and again for the people to turn Out and defend their country. The inattention to his call and the backwardness among the people is unaccountable.

Providence has blessed the American arms with signal success in the defeat of Tarleton and the surprise of George town by Col. Lee with his Legion. If after this advantage you neglect to take the field and suffer the enemy to overrun the country you will deserve the disgrace ever inseparable from (it). Let me conjure you my country man to fly to arms and to repair to headquarters without loss of time and bring with you ten days provisions. You have everything that is dear and valuable at stake. If you will not face the danger your country is inevitably lost. On the contrary if you repair to arms and confine yourselves to the duties of the field Lord Cornwallis must be inevitably ruined. The Continental Army is marching with all possible dispatch from the Pedee (river) to this place; but without your aid their arrival will be of no consequence.

I am sir,

Your humble servant
Nath. Greene

Lt. Col. Hugins.

VII. General strategic situation correspondence mentioning General Davidson:

January 19, 1781

Dear Sir,

Your letter of the 12th & 14th by express was handed to me last night. The letter of the 5th came to hand this day. The express returns immediately which prevents my giving you so much of my chat as I could wish.

A detachment of 400 Virginians Col. Lee's corps of 250 and your regt. Have arrived with some mounts for the Maryland line and I expect 400 more Virginians who are on the road and daily expect large quantities of stores from the northward. The Spaniards have certainly attacked Pensacola: an expedition against St. Augustine will take place this month.

Genl. Phillips is in the neighbourhood (sic) of Petersburg with 2500 men which I hope will arouse the great knife.

Nothing can be undertaken against Lord Cornwallis that will alarm his so much or prevent his attempting to penetrate so effectually as maintaining your position on Santee and Broad river. Genl. Davidson has called out half the militia of Mecklenburg and Roan (Rowan) Counties and has 300 Hillsboro Militia. They are under the orders of General Morgan.

General Sumpter is I believe a man of great ambition – a good officer and very well informed and decided in his (smudged word). I think Genl. Morgan will receive great advantage from him.

A few weeks I hope will put us in a situation to oppose his Lordship in a very respectable manner.

Yours I.B.

Endorsed on back: Major Edwards Giles with Genl. Morgan

-Notes-

Introduction-

[1] Cowan's Ford was sometimes referred to as "McCowan's Ford" (Scots-Irish).
[2] Champ Clark, *The Civil War: Gettysburg: The Confederate High Tide*, (Alexandria: Time-Life Books, 1985), p.10.

Setting the Stage-
[3] Stephenson, Michael, *Patriot Battles: How the War of Independence Was Fought*, (New York: Harper Perennial, 2007), p. 325.

Conrwallis Cometh-

[4] General Morgan was suffering from severe gout at the time, which was a factor in his being replaced by Greene. John Buchanan, *The Road to Guilford Court House* (New York: John Wiley & Sons, Inc., 1997), p.341.
[5] British Orderly Book, (Cornwallis' ADC comments) 1780-1781, Vol. IX. p. 289.
[6] Ramsour's Mill was a nasty engagement between local Loyalists and Whigs forces in June of 1780. The Patriot forces won the day which crippled Loyalist support prior to Cornwallis establishing his camp months later. John Buchanan, *The Road to Guilford Court House* (New York: John Wiley & Sons, Inc., 1997), p.342.
[7] It is believed that one of the British officers peering through the spyglass was actually Cornwallis., Ibid, p.343.
[8] The North Carolina Society Daughters of the Revolution, *The North Carolina Booklet Vol.V, No.4*. (Raleigh: The North Carolina Society Daughters of the Revolution, 1906), p.238.
[9] Ibid, pp.238-239.

[10] Burke Davis, *The Cowpens-Guilford Courthouse Campaign* (New York: J.B. Lippincott Co., 1962), p.79.

[11] The North Carolina Society Daughters of the Revolution. *The North Carolina Booklet Vol.V, No.4.* Raleigh: The North Carolina Society Daughters of the Revolution, 1906. p.241.

[12] Ibid, p. 245.

[13] Note: The letters were rediscovered in the nineteen sixties, a decade after Dr. Chalmers Davidson's noted biography on the general.

[14] Davidson papers: Chalmers Davidson Collection, Davidson College Archives. (See selected transcriptions within this work.)

[15] William Lee Davidson to Nathaniel Greene, 16th January 1781, Chalmers Davidson Collection, Davidson College Archives.

[16] David Schenck, *History of the Invasion of the Carolinas* (Raleigh: Edwards & Broughton Publishers, 1889), p.236.

[17] Nathaniel Greene's letter to Lt. Colonel Hugins, 31 January 1781 Chalmers Davidson Collection, Davidson College Archives.

[18] Note: Buchanan's comments on Tory participation at Ramsour's Mill, *The Road to Guilford Court House* (New York: John Wiley & Sons, Inc., 1997), pp.106-110.

[19] * Also note the map on page 288 of Gen. Joseph Graham's papers. John Buchanan, *The Road to Guilford Court House* (New York: John Wiley & Sons, Inc., 1997), p. 345.

[20] John Shy, *A People Numerous & Armed* (New York: Oxford University Press, 1976), p. 10.

[21] * Believed to be a cousin.

[22] Robert Henry and another local school boy by the name of Charles Rutledge joined the picket and was welcomed…maybe because they brought a pint of whiskey against the cold, as much as two more muskets against the British. Burke Davis, *The Cowpens-Guilford Courthouse Campaign* (New York: J.B. Lippincott Co., 1962), p.80. Also note Henry's full narrative.

[23] Ibid, p.81

[24] Ibid, p.82.

[25] Robert Henry's accounts supports this point, and the strength of the current at the time of the crossing.

[26] John Buchanan, *The Road to Guilford Court House* (New York: John Wiley & Sons, Inc. 1997), p. 347.

[27] Evidently, Beatty died a short time after the initial engagement. Robert Henry, *Narrative of the Battle of Cowan's Ford, February 1ˢᵗ, 1781.*Greensboro: D. Schenck, Sr., 1891, P.11.

[28] Graham narrative: Also note differences in Henry's narrative p.10-12.

[29] Chalmers G. Davidson, *Piedmont Partisan: The Life and Times of General William Lee Davidson*, (Davidson: Davidson College Press, 1951), p.118.

[30] * The numbers were most likely embellished. Daniel Barefoot, *Touring North Carolina's Revolutionary War Sites*, (Winston-Salem: John F. Blair Publisher, 1998.), pp.295-296.

[31] Newsome, A. R., et al., ed. "A British Orderly Book, 1780-1781," *The North Carolina Historical Review*, Vol. IX, 1932.p. 294.

[32] John Buchanan, *The Road to Guilford Court House* (New York: John Wiley & Sons, Inc. 1997), p. 348.

[33] * Robert Henry stated that it was a fellow by the name of Thompson who had built a fishing dam.

[34] Ibid, p. 348.

[35] Gaston C. Davidson, *Piedmont Partisan: The Life and Times of Brigadier-General William Lee Davidson* (Davidson: Davidson Printing Company, 1951), p. 120.

[36] Ibid, pp.120-121.

[37] Also buried at Hopewell are several supposed signers of the Mecklenburg Declaration. * See Daniel W. Barefoot's *Touring North Carolina's Revolutionary War Sites*, (Winston-Salem: John F. Blair Publisher, 1998), pp. 175-177.

Post-Mortem: The Man and the Battle-

[38] For example: Middlekauff's *The Glorious Cause* has but a paragraph, Buchanan's *The Road to Guilford Courthouse* and Morrill's work *Southern Campaigns of the American Revolution* has but a few narrative pages.

[39] Chalmers G. Davidson, *Piedmont Partisan: The Life and Times of General William Lee Davidson*, (Davidson: Davidson College Press, 1951),pp.13-14.

[40] Ibid, p.13.

[41] Henry also notes in his account the number of bodies found in fish traps days later as being drowned with little evidence of their being killed by Patriot musketry.

Banastre Tarleton, *History of the Campaigns of 1780 and 1781 in the Southern Provinces of North America* (London: Cadell Co., 1787), [Reprinted 1968], pp. 224-226.

[42] Walter Clark, ed., *The State Records of North Carolina, vol. XIX,* (Wilmington: Broadfoot Publishing Co., 1994), p. 968.

[43] William Graham, *Gen. Joseph Graham and his Revolutionary Papers*, (Raleigh: Edwards & Broughton, 1904), pp. 288-306.

[44] Alfred F. Young, *The Shoemaker and the Tea Party,* (Boston: Beacon Press, 1999), p. 135.

[45] Robert Henry, *Narrative of the Battle of Cowan's Ford, February 1st, 1781.* Greensboro: D. Schenck, Sr., 1891., p.5.

[46] Ibid, pp.3-4.

[47] Henry specifically dissects Wheelers work and dismisses several points as rubbish. Ibid, p.7.

[48] Dr. Davidson even mentions the disruption of Fourth Creek Presbyterian's church service to call for volunteers prior to the fight. The parson, James Hall, and others marched to support the partisans. A true 'Christian soldiers marching to war' image if there ever was one. Chalmers G. Davidson, *Piedmont Partisan: The Life and Times of General William Lee Davidson*, (Davidson: Davidson College Press, 1951),p.111.

[49] Ibid. p.10.

[50] Ibid, pp.10-11.

[51] Henry's account of the Tory oral tradition was from one Nicholas Gosnell. Gosnell, in what seems to be a bit propagandistic language, almost sings the praises of Beal's deeds in the service of Lord Cornwallis. Ibid, p.13.

[52] * There still exist strong oral traditions (supported by the Hager family) that it was a Hager who was the Tory guide in question. Reportedly, the family moved away westward within hours of the battle for fear of reprisals. Also note: Chalmers G. Davidson, *Piedmont Partisan: The Life and Times of General William Lee Davidson*, (Davidson: Davidson College Press, 1951),p.115.

[53] Clark, June Murtie, *Loyalists in the Southern Campaign of the Revolutionary War*, (Baltimore: Genealogical Publishing Co. Inc., 1981), pp.364-366.

[54] One wonders, like all personal accounts, how accurate the recollection could be after years have passed and heroism seems to cloud youthful events? Ibid, pp.12-13.

Davidson College, the Presbytery and Lasting Legacies-

[55] Concord Presbytery Records, 1832-1836, Vol. 3. North Carolina History of Higher Education Digital Project [Online Collection]. Davidson College Archives. pp.92-97.

[56] Walter Clark, ed., *The State Records of North Carolina, vol. XXII,* (Wilmington: Broadfoot Publishing Co., 1994), pp. 115-117.

[57] Funds were left by the Davidson family to the Presbytery as well. Rev. Robert Hall, "Invocation Speech." Concord Presbytery Records, 1832-1836, Vol. 3. North Carolina History of Higher Education Digital Project [Online Collection]. Davidson College Archives. p. 96.

[58] P.S. Sparrow, "Faculty Address," Concord Presbytery Records, 1832-1836, Vol. 3. North Carolina History of Higher Education Digital Project [Online Collection]. Davidson College Archives. pp. 16-17.

[59] Ibid, pp.23-24.

[60] Hugh T. Lefler and Albert R. Newsome, *History of a Southern State: North Carolina,* (Chapel Hill: The University of North Carolina Press, 1954), p. 400.

[61] Thomas H. Hamilton letter to his brother Davidson, North Carolina History of Higher Education Digital Project [Online Collection]. Davidson College Archives.

[62] John W. Moore, *School History of North Carolina* (New York: American Book Co., 1882), p.134.

[63] Cornelia P. Spencer, *First Steps in North Carolina History, no.1,* (Raleigh: Alfred Williams & Co., 1889), p.140.

[64] For example, see David Schenck, *History of the Invasion of the Carolinas,* (Raleigh: Edwards & Broughton Publishers, 1889)

[65] "Handsome Memorial to Gen. Davidson at Hopewell," *The Davidsonian,* Davidson College Press, (October 8th, 1920), pp.1-8.

[66] Chalmers G. Davidson, *Piedmont Partisan: The Life and Times of General William Lee Davidson,* (Davidson: Davidson College Press, 1951), p.133. Also note the William Lee Davidson Chapter of the DAR Website: http://www.tndar.org-gen eraldavidson/index.htm (Retrieved: 07/07/2011)

The General and the "Mecklenburg Declaration"-

[67] Robert N. Current, "That Other Declaration: May 20, 1775- May 20, 1975," *North Carolina Historical Review*, Vol. LIV, no. 2 (April 1977): 169-170.

[68] Ibid, p. 170.

[69] Ibid, pp. 170-180.

[70] Legette Blythe, "Delay Allowed Greene to Cross Dan and Prepare for Crucial Test at Guilford." *The Charlotte Observer,* August 7th, 1927.

[71] Ibid.

[72] Maude Waddell, "Sent Her Scotch-Irish Sons To Trace Out New Frontiers," *The Charlotte Observer*, August 2nd, 1931.

[73] Ibid.

[74] Ibid.

[75] Ibid.

[76] Interesting side story: Wilson visited his old dorm-room, knocked on the door and the current occupant said "who is it?" The President replied "Woodrow Wilson," the freshman said sarcastically "You've got nothing on me...I'm Christopher Columbus!" Then opened the door and was so shocked that it was the President that he jumped out of the window. Walter L. Lingle, *Memories of Davidson College*, (Richmond: John Knox Press, 1947), p. 104.

[77] Chalmers G. Davidson, *Piedmont Partisan: The Life and Times of General William Lee Davidson*, (Davidson: Davidson College Press, 1951), p. 32.

[78] *Current notes that Chalmers Davidson was the only academic historian willing to say anything positive about the Mecklenburg Declaration during the 1975 celebrations. Robert N. Current, "That Other Declaration: May 20, 1775- May 20, 1975," *North Carolina Historical Review*, Vol. LIV, no. 2, (April 1977): p.190. * Also, Dr. Davidson may have heard stories passed down from within the family itself?

[79] Chalmers G. Davidson, *Piedmont Partisan: The Life and Times of General William Lee Davidson*, (Davidson: Davidson College Press, 1951), p. 124.

[80] Ibid, p.121.

[81] Ibid, pp.122-123.

[82] * The *Charlotte Observer*, Dec. 16th, 1951 gave the book a very favorable review.

[83] LeGette Blythe and Charles R. Brockmann, *Hornets' Nest: The Story of Charlotte and Mecklenburg County*, (Charlotte: McNally, 1961), Jacket cover.

[84] Legette Blythe,"Delay Allowed Greene to Cross Dan and Prepare for Crucial Test at Guilford," *The Charlotte Observer*, Charlotte N.C., August 7th, 1927.

[85] LeGette Blythe and Charles R. Brockmann, *Hornets' Nest: The Story of Charlotte and Mecklenburg County*, (Charlotte: McNally, 1961), p. 16.

[86] Ibid, p.16.

[87] "Historian Recalls Ancestor's Heroics," *The Mooresville Tribune*, [editorial], Mooresville N.C., February 4th, 1971.

[88] * Same story also noted in *The Charlotte Observer,* Charlotte N.C., February 1st, 1971. Ibid.

[89] Ernie Wood, "Minor Battle on Catawba Took Life of N.C. Leader," *The News and Observer*, Raleigh N.C., Sunday, February 8th, 1976.

[90] * Also displayed and photographed at Guildford Court House. www.2davidson.edu/new/news_archieves/archives01/01.06gendavidsonwallet.html   (Retrieved: 07/22/10).

[91] Chalmers G. Davidson, *Piedmont Partisan: The Life and Times of General William Lee Davidson*, (Davidson: Davidson College Press, 1951), p. 125.

[92] Alfred F. Young, *The Shoemaker and the Tea Party*, (Boston: Beacon Press, 1999), p.196.

Changing Times and Future Possibilities-

Author's commentary.

Selected Transcriptions- *Note*: Some of the captured materials that are on file in England from the Davidson Wallet were mixed, I believe, with other captured communications from the Southern Campaign. Several communications within the file post-date the action on the Catawba. (Transcriptions of Gen. Davidson's Letters: US Public Domain)

- Sources -

Babbits, Lawrence E., and Howard, Joshua B. *Long, Obstinate, and Bloody: The Battle of Guilford Courthouse*. Chapel Hill: The University of North Carolina Press, 2009.

Barefoot, Daniel, *Touring North Carolina's Revolutionary War Sites*, Winston-Salem: John F. Blair Publisher, 1998.

Blythe, Legette. "Delay Allowed Greene to Cross Dan and Prepare for Crucial Test at Guilford," *The Charlotte Observer,* 7 August 1927.

_____ , and Charles R. Brockman. *Hornets' Nest: The Story of Charlotte and Mecklenburg County*. Charlotte: McNally, 1961.

Buchanan, John. *The Road to Guilford Court House*. New York: John Wiley & Sons, Inc., 1997.

Clark, Walter., et al., ed. *The State Records of North Carolina,* Vol. XIX. Wilmington: Broadfoot Publishing Co., 1994.

_____ .,. *The State Records of North Carolina,* Vol. XXII. Wilmington: Broadfoot Publishing Co., 1994.

Clark, Champ, *The Civil War: Gettysburg: The Confederate High Tide,* Alexandria: Time-Life Books, 1985.

Clark, June Murtie, *Loyalists in the Southern Campaign of the Revolutionary War*, Baltimore: Genealogical Publishing Co. Inc., 1981.

Concord Presbytery Records, 1832-1836, Vol. 3. North Carolina History of Higher Education Digital Project [Online Collection]. Davidson College Archives.

Current, Robert N. "That Other Declaration: May 20, 1775- May 20, 1975," *North Carolina Historical Review*, Vol. LIV, no.2. April 1977.

Davidson, Chalmers G. *Piedmont Partisan: The Life and Times of General William Lee Davidson*. Davidson: Davidson College Press, 1951.

Davidson, William Lee to Nathaniel Greene, 16th January 1781, Chalmers Davidson Collection, Davidson College Archives.

Davis, Burke. *The Cowpens-Guilford Courthouse Campaign*. New York: J.B. Lippincott Co., 1962.

Graham, William. *Gen. Joseph Graham and his Revolutionary Papers*. Raleigh: Edwards & Broughton, 1904.

Hall, Rev. Robert. "Invocation Speech," 2nd August 1838, North Carolina History of Higher Education Digital Project [Online Collection]. Davidson College Archives.

Hamilton, Thomas H. letter to his brother. 7th October 1837, North Carolina History of Higher Education Digital Project [Online Collection]. Davidson College Archives.

Henry, Robert, *Narrative of the Battle of Cowan's Ford, February 1ˢᵗ, 1781.* Greensboro: D. Schenck, Sr., 1891.

"Historian Recalls Ancestor's Heroics," [editorial], *Mooresville Tribune*, Vol. XXXVII, 4 February 1971.

Lefler, Hugh T. and Albert R. Newsome. *History of a Southern State: North Carolina.* Chapel Hill: The University of North Carolina Press, 1954.

Lingle, Walter. *Memories of Davidson College.* Richmond: Knox Press, 1947.

Lossing, Benson J., Several hundred engravings on wood, by Lossing and Barritt, chiefly from original sketches by the author. New York: Harper & Brothers, 1851-52, C970.3 L87p v. 2. [Image of Cowan's Ford, p. 598] (Courtesy of University of North Carolina Chapel Hill: North Carolina Collections, Wilson Special Collections Library).

Moore, John W. *School History of North Carolina.* New York: American Book Co., 1882.

Newsome, A. R., et al., ed. "A British Orderly Book, 1780-1781," *The North Carolina Historical Review*, Vol. IX, 1932.

O'Kelly, Patrick. *Nothing but Blood and Slaughter: The Revolutionary War in the Carolinas Volume Three 1781*, Bangor: Blue House Tavern Press, 2005.

Schenck, David. *History of the Invasion of the Carolinas.* Raleigh: Edwards & Broughton Publishers, 1889.

Shy, John. *A People Numerous and Armed.* New York: Oxford University Press, 1976.

Sparrow, P.S. "Faculty Address" 2nd August 1838, North Carolina History of Higher Education Digital Project [Online Collection]. Davidson College Archives.

Spencer, Cornelia P. *First Steps in North Carolina History*, no.1. Raleigh: Alfred Williams Co., 1889.

Stephenson, Michael, *Patriot Battles: How the War of Independence Was Fought*, New York: Harper Perennial, 2007.

Swisher, James K., *The Revolutionary War in the Southern Back Country*, Gretna: Pelican Publishing Company, 2008.

Tarleton, Banastre, *History of the Campaigns of 1780 and 1781 in the Southern Provinces of North America*. London: Cadell Co., 1787. Reprinted: 1968.

Waddell, Maude. "Sent Her Scotch-Irish Sons to Trace Out New Frontiers," *The Charlotte Observer*, 2 August 1931.

Wood, Ernie. "Minor Battle on Catawba Took Life of N.C. Leader," *The News and Observer*, 8 February 1976.

Young, Alfred F. *The Shoemaker and the Tea Party*. Boston: Beacon Press, 1999.

Online Sources-

Davidson College Website: *Archive:* http://www2.davidson.edu/news/
news_archives/archives01/01.06gendavidsonwallet.html (Information
Retrieved 07/22/2010)

William Lee Davidson Chapter of the DAR Website: http://www.tndar.
org-generaldavidson/index.htm (Information Retrieved: 07/07/2011)

Made in the USA
Middletown, DE
22 December 2022

17410380R00047